The Song of Life

100 Random Poems

By

Peyush Gurung

Shield  Crest

© Copyright 2017 Peyush Gurung

All rights reserved

This book shall not, by way of trade or otherwise, be lent, re-sold, hired out, or otherwise circulated without the prior consent of the copyright holder or the publisher in any form of binding or cover other than that in which it is published and without a similar condition including this condition being imposed on the subsequent purchaser. The use of its contents in any other media is also subject to the same conditions.

ISBN: 978-1-911090-68-7

MMXVII

A CIP catalogue record for this book
is available from the British Library

Published by
ShieldCrest Publishing Ltd.,
Aylesbury, Buckinghamshire,
HP22 5RR England
Tel: +44 (0) 333 8000 890
www.shieldcrest.co.uk

Dedications

To my mum for raising me up and making me the person I am today.

Also, to the rest of my family. Though they weren't always there, they still supported me during the making of this poem book.

And apologies to my friends at Coombes CE Primary and Holy Trinity CE School who I lost contact with.

Acknowledgment

To my dad for supporting me in the making of this book and directing me on what to do and what not to do.

Also to the people at ShieldCrest Publishing for helping me to publish the book.

Contents

Royal Family 1

Limerick of Love 2

The Story of Life 3

Britain 4

Jelly Baby 6

Nuclear Bomb 7

Earth 8

Religion 9

Addiction 10

Childhood 11

Boys 12

Girls 14

Gold Heart 16

Luckiness 17

Sky 18

Gaming 19

Human Body 20

Chocolate 22

Studying 23

Animals 24

The Earthquake That Shook Nepal	26
Snow	28
Angels	29
Germs	30
I'm Mad and Bad	31
Christmas	32
Chinese New Year	34
Mirror	35
Time	36
The Night Sky	38
The Oven	39
River of Many Kinds	40
Strongest Man	42
Happy-ish	43
Mountain Strength	44
Hour of Need	45
Soul	46
Pillow	48
Radio	49
Human as Popcorn	50
The Void	51
Limerick	52

The Human Heart	53
Aliens of a Different Kind	54
Gangster Tortoise	55
Party to Die For	56
Magic Within a Human	57
Forest	58
Rainbow	59
Dictionary	60
Lav	61
Little Little Fishy	62
Sweets and Candy	63
The Song of Life	64
Music	66
School's Very Good	67
Birds	68
The Human Mind	70
Cats	71
Dogs	72
Camera	73
Hooded Man	74
School Days	75
59	76

Heads or Tails 77

Week 78

Summer 80

My Garden 81

The 'Green Giant' 82

People 85

Over the horizon 86

Eyes 88

The Future of Nature 89

Model Village 90

Footy 92

Floral 93

BBQ 94

Green Park 96

Relationships 97

Space 98

This Website YouTube 99

Shopping 100

Funny! 102

Smile 103

Nation 104

Travel 105

Television	106
Mother's Day	108
After Pollution	109
Buddha	110
A Rhyme	112
Volcanic Eruptions	113
See the Sea	114
War	116
My 'Rap'	118
Gun	119
Tornado	120
Teddy Bear	122
Peace	123
Best Friend	124
About the Author	126

Peyush Gurung

Royal Family

The Royal family
Deserves loyalty
They keep the country in order
By repelling dangers of the border

They must be posh
Their life should be so lush
Or are they energetic like us
Doing everything in a rush?

They probably don't have time to have fun
Not enough to have a jolly run
They must work intensely
They seem to have fun hardly

So, listen loud and clear
Can you hear?
It would be nice to help out
With whatever they're about

The Song of Life

Limerick of Love

We fit well together

We could live forever

Because the most impossible

Is the possible

Whenever I'm with you

Just like PB and J

Works well together

And I wouldn't miss a day

For that beautiful smile

Even if I'll have to

Walk a million miles

Peyush Gurung

The Story of Life

Once was a person
Born into a world
Shrouded with mystery
Waiting for its story to unfold

The person grew older
And became taller
Went on to make many friends
But that's where his life bends

Life as he knew it went fast
Days were short
And started to pass

Became more weaker
Than stronger

And finally, it came to an end
And no longer needed to wend

The Song of Life

Britain

We enjoy our tea

Nice and sugary

And our crumpets

All nice and toasty

We all love our country

And every county

We go

We honour our Queen

No matter how old

She always will be evergreen

Like a lion, we roar!

Like an eagle, we'll soar!

We all love a great time down the pub

With the free BT-hub

And the old chippy

Where there are chips and fish

an exquisite dish

Peyush Gurung

I love Britain
And that's swell

The Union Jack
Our colourful flag
Red, blue and white
Signifying might
Also, our right

The combination
Of every country
Scotland, England and Wales
Each jam-packed with awesome tales

Oh, I say, we're British and proud
And don't mind if we get a bit too loud

The Song of Life

Jelly Baby

I was made in England

I'm the bestselling brand

I am a dummy

I have no mummy

Because I'm made out of gummy

This is crazy

I know I'm tasty

Many flavours to choose from

Well, maybe not bubble gum

I'm sweet as a plum

I'm chewy like gum

They eat me with glee

Although I try to flee

Because I want to be free

Peyush Gurung

Nuclear Bomb

It's powerful
That's undeniable
Poisonous radioactivity
A killer activity

You won't escape in time
As you hear the ticking chime

When it blows
There will be an up-rising

Skies will rumble
The ground will tremble

But they won't release the blow
They're scared of releasing the flow
Flow of bombs down and down
Because that'll start a war
A world war. . .

The Song of Life

Earth

Earth is full of life
But it's deadlier than a knife
So far, it's only one
That has many lives on

If pollution is done
Earth will soon be gone
Once where life shone
It will disappear

And the world will be clear
With nothing to fear
Earth is our home
It's like a protective dome

Our species is growing
Our earth is dying
We don't own Earth
Earth gave us birth!

Peyush Gurung

Religion

Religion
Affects fashion
Religion
Comes with tradition

Fills people with determination
It'll bring bad things to extinction
It brings us closer

But some use excuses
Like ISIS
But we can stop this
No matter how difficult it is

Violence leads to more violence
Hence
The reason for bombings
And things exploding

Half of the population lost
Never to be found again

The Song of Life

Addiction

Addiction is bad
And it's so sad
Because it drives people mad
Have no addiction, just be glad

There are many types of addiction
Like drinking alcoholic drinks
That'll make your breath stink

Also, playing a game
Parents ashamed

Addiction to money
This is kind of funny

And smoking
Can be very injuring

But you'll go crazy
And maybe a bit hazy
If you don't have it all the time

I'm off
To do some mysterious stuff

Peyush Gurung

Childhood

Childhood can be a blast
But it goes too fast

True that in childhood
We mostly drink and eat food

But we mostly explored
To keep ourselves from being bored

It was the one chance of having freedom

We don't care for money
We find it funny
Because we share
And care

But the economy
Acts like an enemy
To each other

The Song of Life

Boys

Little boys
Like cool toys

Older boys
Search for fame
By playing a game

And male adults
Are just boring

But all boys are similar
Besides not looking familiar
Boys will be boys

Rough and tough
Mean and lean
But some are caring
And very sharing

Peyush Gurung

Sure, there are disagreements
And big fights
But we are intellectual
And we all know best

Girls

Girls are

Well . . . dunno

Sometimes they're nice

Sometimes they're aggressive

And their words are soft

But can also be corrosive

Unlike men they're very pretty

But also unlike men

Extremely chatty

They love fashion

It's like passion

Similar to a man

And his football

They're a backbone

To men

Without them

Society would collapse

Peyush Gurung

But what do I know, I'm just
Writing about girls
Even though I don't know a single thing about them

The Song of Life

Gold Heart

A gold heart
A kindred spirit
Always happy
Not at all snappy

Calm with everything
Helps anyone
And anything

No stress, no pain
And does things very humane

Innocence
And kindness
And kindness

Minus
The fact
A gold heart isn't
Possible

Peyush Gurung

Luckiness

It's so cool

To be lucky

Everything happens to be good

It makes me feel safe

Not at all unsafe

It brings fortune

Yay, no misfortune!

It gives me money

Don't worry

I'm not crazy

The Song of Life

Sky

The sky

It's so up high

And it's where birds fly

And where the clouds go to cry

The sky can get dark

Filling it with stark

Zeus does a big call

It's the day and night

Both dark and bright

It's like a waterfall

The sky

The sky

It's so wonderful

And blue-tiful

Peyush Gurung

Gaming

It's a big thing

Makes easy cash
And spreads like a rash

Some do it for entertainment
Some do it for employment

A time-passer
An excuse for a gamer
A universe full of excitement
A world with no loneliness

Explore deep caverns
Simulate as ravens

Do anything
Be everything
Because it's your world
For everything to be told

The Song of Life

Human Body

The human body
Is amazing

It makes us live
And thrive
It has multiple cells
That makes up tissue
Which holds it in place like glue

Tissues to make up organs
Working like an orchestra
And organs make a body
The body is complicated
That even scientists get frustrated

The veins thinner than paper
Carries blood cells
Smaller than dust

One drop containing a million
So, there should be a trillion
Or even a gazillion

It makes us an organism
All of us are the same
But, of course, in the inside
Or it might be a little lame

Outside we're different
But together we make a civilisation
And a civilisation all together is a country
Then countries together make a continent
And we should take care of it and our body
What I'm trying to say is
The world is our body
We're all cells in a way
All that conflict is sickness
And continents make a world

The Song of Life

Chocolate

Chocolate is yummy
It satisfies my tummy
Made out of milk
As white as silk

Some are sugary
All are dairy
Some are healthy
And most are unhealthy

Some have great quality
And some are made awfully
Some are dark and white
But I don't care which to bite

If only it grew on a trees
I'd pick it everyday
Monday all the way to Friday

Peyush Gurung

Studying

Education
Gets your brain in function
It takes you far

Makes you smart
That you're sharper than a dart

So many types of education
There's one for fashion
Music sessions
With instruments at your possession
Many art creations
And science with explosions

You'll be thankful
And to the teachers grateful
Your parents would be proud
And others will say your name out loud

The Song of Life

Animals

Some are more civilised
But they've all survived
Most had to be killed

Most are smart
Most have feelings and heart
That's how they adapt
It's like a curse
Good or bad

To support different evolution phases
And to form different faces

Predators
Are hunters
With slashing jaws
And sharp claws

Prey

Are left to pray

As they are hunted

But they have defences and brains

Animals will kill

To live

And thrive

And whether they

Live or die

The Song of Life

The Earthquake That Shook Nepal

In April 2015
A terrible
Earthquake occurred

A tragic event
That left the peoples
Living on streets
And in shelter tents

7.8 magnitude
Shattered the earth
With a ferocious
Attitude

It killed 9,000 people
Injured 22,000
And destroyed religious temples

Many people were lost
And it came with
A great cost

Families were torn apart
And people driven to madness
Exceeding the bar chart
It struck them
And they couldn't do
Anything to help
But all they did was hear
The scary high-pitch yelp

The Song of Life

Snow

Snow

So white

Spread across the ground

Lovely and beautifully

Sometimes a nuisance

But also

You might find it inducing

Having snowball fights

Is fun and enraging

So many fun activities

Like snowmen

Snow angels

Snow forts

Peyush Gurung

<u>Angels</u>

Angels have wings
And they have
Halo rings
Voices like no other
Like a lullaby from a mother

They're peaceful
And have no aggression
And that's why most
Don't feel sorrow and
Depression

As nothing is a bother

Germs

Germs are everywhere
In your toes
In your nose
And in your hair

Germs are miniscule
Tiny but powerful
Something not to be ridiculed

As germs can lead to disease
Disease leads to viruses
And viruses lead to a death increase

Peyush Gurung

I'm Mad and Bad

I'm mad and bad
I'm bad and mad

I'm mad
Because everything that I've ever owned
Everything that I've ever had
Is gone, I'm done
It's not okay
I'm in dismay

I'm mad and bad
I'm bad and mad

I'm bad

The Song of Life

Christmas

Holly bushes
Very prickly
Green, lovely-scented
Pine tree

The way life
Becomes lively
Well, everything's
Perfect on Christmas Eve

Families gathering
Around the table
Children hyperactive
And unstable

Happy faces everywhere
Sad faces
To be seen are
Nowhere

Peyush Gurung

Again everything
Is perfect on Christmas Eve
If everything's wrong
It's a misconceive

The Song of Life

Chinese New Year

Red and yellow
Everywhere
Things with a golden glow

With an aroma
Of lovely curry
I see them trying to get it
In a hurry

Lucky children in line
Waiting for money
As I figure out a rhyme
Oh, there we go

As the noise of excitement grows
So does the parade

Dragons dancing majestically
And people on floats
Also dancing, but frantically

It feels great to be in a big crowd

Peyush Gurung

Mirror

The mirror tells the truth
Making you feel happy
Or a bit ruth

Whether you think you look pretty
Or a bit unwitty
No matter if you're tall or small
Fat or slim
The mirror will show you

Whether you're angry
At the outcome
Whether you look blankly
At the outcome
Or you think it's dandy
Because of the outcome
The mirror will always be true

And would probably always
Show the true you

Time

Time doesn't stop

Not for you

For me

Or anybody

It goes quickly

It goes slowly

For it is time

A key element of an organized crime

A ripening of a lime

Oxidation of a dime

And the time I spent

Figuring out a rhyme

Time is priceless

And I'm not talking bias

As time can't be bought
Or sold

Because it's already with you
And never will leave

The Song of Life

The Night Sky

All dark and majestic

The night sky

Calm and domestic

The night sky

Lit up with millions of stars

The night sky

Many planets such as Mars

The night sky

Full of materials and substance

The night sky

And most aren't discovered, trust us

Home to the unknown

The night sky

The dark has grown

Blacker than the blackest of black

The night sky

Blacker, better, blacker is better

And every night it comes back

Peyush Gurung

The Oven

The oven

A useful tool
To cook your food
And it can burn stuff
So, stay aware
Or you might look like a fool

It heats up
To an unimaginable fire
Turn the knob
Make it even higher

Put anything in it
Even if it can't fit

Nuke it up
Raise the flames
Take it out of the oven
What do you get?

A 5-star meal

The Song of Life

River of Many Kinds

A river

Is like a celebrity

Though they die

Their names live long

Like a song

Overused and dried up

But it's still real

A river

Has a start and never ends

Who knows how much time

It has to spend

And even though it might

Have a start or end

It will keep on going

Making trees and plants

Growing

Peyush Gurung

Makes many people relaxed
By sitting and enjoying the view
Long and streaky
And oh, so blue

The Song of Life

Strongest Man

The wars of wars
The fights of fights

Reaching to the greatest heights

To proclaim the name
Of the strongest man

But only the man who
Is the strongest
Shall proclaim the name
The Strongest Man

You need the muscles
But also brains
Mostly muscles

Peyush Gurung

Happy-ish

Be happy
Not sad
Don't care if you're happy-ish

Be joyful
Not depressed
Or just happy-ish

Funny
But not a fool
A clown fish

Accepted
But no failure
So, you should be
Happy not wish

The Song of Life

Mountain Strength

It's tall

And

Greater than a wall

It stretches above

Touching the sky

Looking always a bit

"Bone-dry"

Many risk lives

To climb many of these giants

Which is fierce and defiant

It's big

It's strong

It's amazing

It's a mountain

Peyush Gurung

Hour of Need

Hour by hour
We lose power

Our motivation
Depletes
Making us do less
Good actions

Hour by hour
Hope dies
As you can hear
The people's cries

And what am I saying
Well, it's called praying
For the world
To stop the cruel fighting

Soul

Soul

Is what we all have and need

To grow strong

Like a seed

To a tree

Soul is

Within us

And what makes us unique

Now let's discuss

The speciality of our soul

A soul

Makes us whole

A soul is the key thing

For us to love and hate

A soul

Decides our fate

And our current state

It is a life-giver
A life-shower
A life-learner
And all

The Song of Life

Pillow

A use of comfort
And decoration
It looks like a
Pillow deformation

Comes in a wide variety
And can give out
Someone's personality

Soft, hard, or prickly
It's your choice

Smooth
Enough to make you soothe
Fluffy, puffy
And very "stuffy"

Pink, red
Handmade
Blue, black
Just like a sack

Peyush Gurung

Radio

The static noise
Tuned to perfection
Producing a song
Putting our hips in motion

Electronic power
Made to a voice
Of your choice

A huge panel
For a channel
Directed to people
By radio signals

The Song of Life

Human as Popcorn

Men and woman alike
Are like popcorn
They're born
And through the heat
That is hate
Comes out a new person

Peyush Gurung

The Void

Black and empty
Nothing like cold Pepsi
Not unlike a portal
Or even a black hole

But dangerous
Even for the willing
And adventurous

Will of nothing and space
That goes on for miles and more
Or
Even more

The Song of Life

Limerick

This is a limerick

Made by a poet

Who is eating

A mullet

He was going to eat a McFillet

But he was in a McFlurry

As the line was long

And he was in a worry

The situation got a bit hairy

Like Chewbacca

The cat spat

Had just spat

A hairball

This was a poem

A limerick poem

And the worst of all

Peyush Gurung

<u>The Human Heart</u>

The heart
Mystery to the smartest of people

Jerks uncontrollably
And supplies
The blood to the body

A ball of muscle
Functions
Like it's in a tussle

The Song of Life

Aliens of a Different Kind

Hello, we come in cheese

We rope you do too

We've been watching over shoe

For abominations

And learning your language

For treasuries

There are so many rows

But we kept with the Ramen language

Which is English

Transition out

Peyush Gurung

Gangster Tortoise

I am the tortoise that never stops
Not even for the cops
But then again, they never catch me in the act
And that's a fact

I'm slow as a snail
My reputation is bigger than a whale
My bullets hurt like hail
Did I mention I'm cold as one?
So, I can break your heart, Hun?

You better run
Because I might blow

But you've got time
Cause I'm very slo--ow

The Song of Life

Party to Die For

I love a good old-fashioned party
Full of joy and people all hearty
Now come along
And don't be a smarty

Or I'll take you in
For a spin
In my luxurious blender
Sorry to offend ya

Now join me
Join them
They've been waiting for you

But there's also
In store for you, too . . .

Peyush Gurung

Magic Within a Human

Magic
Is all around us

From our hands
To our feet

Our will and determination
Our love and compassion
Human minds
Binds

With the knowledge of past and presence
Bringing the future with every step

That's magic

The Song of Life

Forest

Scary but beautiful
But never always full

Always busy and lively
With many plants and critters
Making it dirty and winter

Though it's beautiful
People won't stop
Cutting trees down

They supply our oxygen
That helps us humans

And the animal's home
Destroyed and no more
They are only left to roam

Peyush Gurung

Rainbow

Vibrant, colourful
And beautiful

Way up in the sky
Where most birds fly

At the end of a rainbow
There's a pot of gold
But the myth's pretty old

The Song of Life

Dictionary

Full of words

Gathered in one place

Just like herds

Know your knowledge

Make yourself "cutting edge"

With pages and pages

With many

Words of many ages

Thick layers

Made from many acres

And many makers

Peyush Gurung

Lav

What is a lav?
Well, it's something you have

It's like a big bowl
But not something you eat from

In your house
Up the stair
Put your hand in it if you dare

It's where the foulest things happen
And to clean this thing
It isn't much fun

It's called a lav for a reason
Because it's short for something
And that is lavatory

Yep, a lav is a toilet

The Song of Life

Little Little Fishy

Little fishy

Swimming in the water

Of which **alma mater**

Have you come from?

Little fishy

Oh, so blue

Just like the water

Almost see-through

Little fishy

I need to go

Go swim

To the depths below

Bye-bye

Little fishy!

Peyush Gurung

Sweets and Candy

Sweet, sweets
Sweeter than
A cool song beats

Sweets, sweets
If you're outdated
You'll smell like feet

Candy, candy
Sour as brandy

Candy, candy
You're quite dandy

Sweets, candy
Both the same
It's just the name

The Song of Life

The Song of Life

You're born

Into a vast world

Always trying to fit in

Or you'll be treated like a trash bin

Getting bullied but

You'll pull through

The only way you'll ever know

Is to be put into their shoes

No matter if you're

Rich or poor

There's always going to be a locked door

War and hunger

Have driven us apart

So, let's just forget about the past

Growing up

You'll learn a lot

So, whatever comes up, take a shot

Getting a husband and wife
There's still more
Like your children to adore

This is the song of life
Relationships
Hardships
Responsibility
A good identity

The Song of Life

Music

It can be beautiful
And colourful

There is variety of songs
Short and long

Music can move you
You know it's true

There can be many types
Like classical
And rapping
Some comedic
But nearly every song is fantastic

Use your ears
Turning on each of your gears
Because it's music

Peyush Gurung

School's Very Good

It's an amazing place
With unique faces

Learning new things
Almost every day
With teachers
Strict or nice

Making friends
Or enemies
But that's partially OK

I like art
That's a start
I like cooking
And making tarts

I like learning new languages
Such as French and Spanish

But it's mostly the end of the day
Because we get to go home!

The Song of Life

Birds

There are all type of birds
Tall, small
Thin, fat
Even fatter or flat
Ones that like the dark
Ones that like the sun
But the both are fun
Some that run because they can't fly
Some that zoom across the sky

Big and dangerous
Small and feeble
Or
Small and dangerous
Big and feeble
Various colours
Black, pink, pink, red and white
Looking for a fight
Watch out they'll strike you
With beauty and might

They'll travel around
Crazy like a hound
To different places
Meeting new faces
This is called migration
A complicated action

They're birds. How many?
A lot

The Song of Life

The Human Mind

The mind

It's an elaborate structure

A body instructor

It helps us with everyday life

Like figuring out puzzles

Or tensing muscles

Like a computer

Full of information

Putting us in motion

We use it everyday

When we work a lot

Or play

Our mind is great

Thinking at alarming rate

It's cool and awesome

Peyush Gurung

<u>Cats</u>

Cats can come in all types of shades
Tabby, white, black or brown
With a smile or a frown

Cute and cuddly
Fat and flabby

An annoyance
Making some people furious
Just because it's curious
Then again, it did kill the cat

But they win our hearts
And secretly control our lives
Becoming slaves in the process . . .

Joking
That would be impossible
Well, I think

The Song of Life

<u>Dogs</u>

Dogs are epic
They're four-legged
And fluffy-headed

They're also sharp-toothed
Eyes cute and round

They're great companions
And athletic, like Olympic champions

Fun to hang with
Because they're man's best friend

Pugs and Corgis an ongoing trend
Poodles fluffy and puffy
Golden Retrievers shiny-coated
And Bulldogs looking bloated

Nice dogs

Peyush Gurung

Camera

I'll take a picture
With it

To show all my friends
How good my camera lenses
Are

I love what I take with it
Even though it comes out
8-bit

I like to take videos
Even though
It's very slow
The frames are slower than a tortoise

It's ~~revolutionary~~
It's fantastic
It's compact
It's . . .
Kind of outdated

The Song of Life

Hooded Man

The hooded man

Doesn't reveal his face

The hooded man

Leaves without a trace

The hooded man

Dives with grace

The hooded man

Can beat any race

The hooded man

Can fly to space

The hooded man

His name is Dan

The hooded man

Peyush Gurung

School Days

Tick, tock, tick
Time's going slow
Ring, ring, ring
It's time to go

It's recess
And I gobble down
My Reese's pieces

Ring, ring
That sound's an unpleasant thing

As I drag myself
To class

I remember it's Friday
And a half-day!
Yay!

59

This is a number

Most specifically

59

And it also rhymes with spine

But there's one more thing

Look up

This is the poem number 59

The 59th poem of this book

But what does that mean?

What does this whole poem mean?

I'll leave the thinking to you

And let your imagination run wild . . .

Peyush Gurung

Heads or Tails

The coin flips
And shakes like it has hips

Everyone's looking
Everyone's staring
They can't take the suspense

Spinning, spinning, spinning
Still spinning

It drops
It plops
Into the gutter
What a huge bummer

The Song of Life

Week

Monday starts
And you're all bummed
Whatever the day holds
You'll be taken away

Then next comes Tuesday
Another hard day
At least after this
You get to hit the hay

Wednesday
Nearly halfway through
Starting to be blue

Thursday
More quickly
Now it's Friday

Finally
I can spend the day happily

Peyush Gurung

With the weekend coming

Saturday and Sunday

Summer

Summer
Isn't always a bummer
But it is going to be hot
Hot enough to sleep on the spot
If you feel dizzy
Drink something cold and fizzy
And the sun will make you sweat
Enough to make you wet
Go outside, get a nice tan
Take something cold, like a fan
And enjoy it while you can
Because it'll go fast
Just like a ball
Rolling off a steep hill

Peyush Gurung

My Garden

My garden is fabulous
With birds so gracious
But they can be mischievous

It's minty fresh
Just like our flowers
Withholding its
Radical superpowers

It's got mysterious species
Other herbs and spices
And fruit/veggies

I don't want to boast
Because I'm
Technically your host

But I bet my garden's better than yours

The Song of Life

The 'Green Giant'

The hill

Nature's tower

And as beautiful as a flower

It's a great view

When the sky's all blue

And clouds are white

Looking all right

It's good for hiking

And striking

Strikingly hard to climb

It holds animals

Mostly mammals

And little birds, too

It can be crowded with trees

And little bees

Peyush Gurung

The sun will be shining
Making it boiling
But the air will still blow
Making heat go

People climb on
Having fun, a ton
While the sun shone

Seeing everything
That's happening
Is very breath-taking

The people all have a smile
Furthermore
Laughing for a while

The hill
So green
Glowing like toxic ooze

The Song of Life

It can be steep
Or on the flat side
Both still thick and wide

Some might even be little bumps
Children call a "hill"
Or big ones rock climbers call a cliff

But something in common to hills
Is that
We're the ones to overcome
This obstacle
That is a hill

That is all

Peyush Gurung

People

People, humans
Fathers, mothers
Sons, daughters

All with a story
All with an alibi

Both good and bad

People of many races
Many religions
Many nations
And in many relationships

One thing in common
Though they are all different
That they are from Earth
And this is our home
In space

Even if we're alone . . .

The Song of Life

Over the horizon

The view is

Breathtaking

How the ground

Meets the sky

It could almost make

A man cry

The towers piercing

The night sky

Stands proud and high

Stars shine

What a holy sight

Over the horizon

Beauty waits

Maybe destiny

Maybe even fate

Peyush Gurung

Over the horizon
Is where we'll go
Even though
We don't know
What awaits.

Eyes

Eyes make you see
See clearly
And freely

Eyes can have rarity
To differ personality

Eyes are a lot
Without them it'll be dark

You <u>see</u>
Eyes are important

Peyush Gurung

The Future of Nature

In the future
There won't be any nature
Because of pollution
It'll stop green function

And will cause more destruction
So, protect the forest
And make it our dearest
And our planet will be the greatest

Our world will cause more devastating
The future won't be that welcoming
There will be radiated food
But it won't really taste good

The Song of Life

Model Village

A model village
Handcrafted to perfection
So strong it withstands destruction
Well, not that much

The detail to the painting
Is so amazing
It's like the real deal
Makes you feel like a giant

The people
Each in their own world
Have a story to tell

Like a robber in a horse race
Why is he there?
A cat stuck on a roof
How did it get there?

Peyush Gurung

It made me feel giant
And also forget how small I am
Compared to the universe

The Song of Life

Footy

Football is great

You can play with all your mates

First, you'll need a ball

And a pitch or hall

Now some players

Hopefully no fouler

So, if you're a referee keep your eyes out

And look about

It's international

And tactical

It's unbeatable

Its unbearable

Well, for me

I prefer to watch

The ongoing match

Peyush Gurung

<u>Floral</u>

A flower is
A small tower
Using the sun for power

Flowers bloom with colour
And are greener than any dollar
Every day they grow taller

The bees make honey
To help its colony
They take nectar
From the flower

So the pollen
Can be spread afar

The Song of Life

BBQ

I had a BBQ
And that's true

The crispy taste
And the silky paste
Gone together like a mix

And crunchy outside
Soft inside

The ketchup red as blood
Spread like a flood

Sun shining
Birds flying
Flowers blooming
And the grill smoking

The burger is nice
And I've just finished my thrice

Peyush Gurung

That's all
Need to go

The Song of Life

Green Park

The royal park

Will never turn dark

Because nature is beautiful

And the park is wonderful

It's mystical

And the structures are historical

The park is a heap of passion

The park has much celebration

Many things to explore

And sights better than a tor

In spring the flowers are exotic

The water park is aquatic

And is very peaceful

I love it there

Peyush Gurung

<u>Relationships</u>

A relationship
Is like a voyage on a ship

It's happy
But can be soppy

It can make you mad
Or sad
It can make you glad
A happy lad

It can thaw a heart of ice
To become nice

The Song of Life

<u>Space</u>

Space
Is deadlier than a mace
But it's ace

And its ginormous
It has a great mass
It holds many planets
In an intergalactic net

Holds a strand of galaxies
And it's our destiny
To discover life
Beyond Earth we'll strive

Space is delusional
As well as fantastical
It has grace
And it is SPACE!

Peyush Gurung

This Website YouTube

YouTube is awesome
I like it a wholesome

Founded by Steve Chen
Chad Hurley
And Jawed Karim
Who I've got to give credit
Because they're a great team

It's like a mini show
That you can watch
In the comfort of your house
Or on the go
With your spouse
Your mum
Your dad
Or your pet mouse
Well, it is for everyone
Because its
Worldwide . . .

The Song of Life

Shopping

Shopping
Can be annoying
Some prices are rising
And some are lowering

More toys
Means girls and boys!
And many parent complaints

Some shops sell clothes
Some sell flowers
Such as daisies and roses
Or gaming consoles

Some shops are beneficial
And some buys are sensational
Some products
Can be fake
They want your money
For them to take

Peyush Gurung

So, use it wisely
The fact that you'll listen
Is very unlikely

The Song of Life

Funny!

Some things are funny
Things that are "Looney"
And also silly

Jokes are funny
Like knock-knock
Or why did the chicken walk

Being funny
Makes new friends
It's really great
And could probably help
You on a date

Making jokes can be a blast
It makes you feel
The opposite of a downcast

But you won't understand
Because understanding would be sitting

Peyush Gurung

Smile

Smiling shows happiness
It eliminates sadness
It fills us with joy
Like a new day

The feeling of winning
Is thrilling
And when you lose
You have the pride of trying

It can be overwhelming
And fulfilling
And no one is harmed by saying a happy
HELLO!

The Song of Life

<u>Nation</u>

A nation full of people
Of different races
Living at different places
And many different faces

Altogether to make up as one
Civilisation evolved quickly
Look how we've done

A nation of people
Of many religions
Tame and calm
Like a domestic pigeon

The government controls us
With arguments with sides
That makes us fuss

Peyush Gurung

<u>Travel</u>

Travelling gets you far
Even more further than a car
But not to the stars

The world becomes clear
As you are near
You'll come face to face with your fear
You can travel in a pair

To make things a bit fair
But if you want to share
Don't you dare
See if they care

The Song of Life

<u>Television</u>

TV is popular
But makes people lazier
The news is helpful
But it can be bad or wonderful
You can be entertained
And it's all arranged
There are many shows
That no one knows

It was first displayed
The year 1927
People got accession
To many shows

Modern television
Was made by Taylor Farnsworth

Thanks to him we have many decisions
Of the TV shows

Peyush Gurung

It will help you shop
It's exciting, you might pop!
Go get them
With no condemn

The Song of Life

Mother's Day

Happy Mother's Day
I'm saying this with no dismay
Unless its attention you don't pay
And good mums should stay

She does our feeding
And does our cleaning
Mums are beautiful,
And also wonderful

She is incredible
But she isn't unbearable
My mum's so humble
So am hoping her life will not crumble

Peyush Gurung

After Pollution

It's a silent day

No one is out to play

The skies are grey

I used to see people shopping away

The streets used to be busy

Know it makes us feel dizzy

Living isn't easy

Because it's cold and very breezy

Children stopped learning

Priests aren't preaching

People are in hiding

Food they are seeking

And surviving

The Song of Life

Buddha

Buddha
Known as
Siddhartha Gautama

Was a lead
Role of Buddhism
And the leader
Of the Buddhist religion

He was born in Nepal
And his figure was tall

He was born
In 567BC
He's like a hero
From Marvel and DC

He was a great motivator
His speeches as followed

Peyush Gurung

"Peace comes within
Do not seek it without"
That is no doubt

"Three things cannot be hidden:
The sun, the moon and the truth"
Just like Chef Ramsay
And his way with food
He was a great teacher
And also a high preacher

A Rhyme

A rhyme

Is like a hymn

Words which are the same

Must remain

The same words

Which are in tune like clanging swords

Some don't rhyme, like orange

And door hinge

But they do sound the same

So, you can't blame

I can't find a rhyming sentence lame

I should have shame

Peyush Gurung

Volcanic Eruptions

They're dangerous
That's for sure
And can destroy
And endanger us

Its stormy clouds
Suffocating
Like massive crowd

It burst with
The colours
Of anger
Orange, yellow and red
Dealing with it
Could lead us dead

But on the bright side
It provides nutrients
To the soil
Leave it unspoiled

The Song of Life

See the Sea

With my eyes I see

The far, far seas

Blue and green

Just like a forest of trees

And with these eyes

I can see

Two dolphins playing

And whales spraying

Water over the horizon

I can smell

The salty water

Burning the back of my throat

And all the smelly fish

On my boat

I can feel the air

Whipping my face

It was a feeling I couldn't bare

Peyush Gurung

But I can't really taste
Anything
Besides the awful smell
Which is fish paste

The Song of Life

War

It's an armed conflict
That can cause
Pain and sadness
Everything goes to madness

As they die in action
Leaving many in a distraught
And a tormented reaction

Some are injured
Losing arms, legs and more
Something even worse
And full of gore

People do die
But it's the way of life
And there'll
Be tears
Be people in fear

Peyush Gurung

There'll be blood
And people
Digging graves in mud

But one thing will
Come out of this
Peace

The Song of Life

My 'Rap'

With the crew
At the back
Nothing can stop us

Got the guns loaded
And ready to shoot
You better watch out
Because I don't give a hoot

I scare people when I say
"GET OVER HERE"
Make a crocodile cry
Crocodile tear
And make a tiger quiver in fear

My mind's sharp
Sharp as a spear

So, you have many reasons
To stop
Grinding my gears

Peyush Gurung

Gun

A gun goes bang, batang and boom. It's deadly
And ready, focusing on the kill, filled with thrill
The bullet goes fast, and zooms past
And an ear-piercing noise is made
As it penetrates the skin
It makes the littlest spin

The Song of Life

Tornado

A tornado is a
Ferocious force
And it destroys anything
Wherever it goes

It spins
Like a cyclone
And travels across the land
Like a big drone

It's common on western
Sides of the world
And less
On the eastern

But tornadoes are
A very serious matter
Because they can
Destroy homes
And causes families to scatter

Peyush Gurung

So be safe when it
Comes to tornadoes

The Song of Life

Teddy Bear

"Teddy bear, oh so sweet"
"You lift me off of my feet"
Not literally
"The adventures we go to"
"And the things we do"

"Please don't leave me"

Peyush Gurung

Peace

It's what we all need
Besides all the war and greed

Every slave to be freed
Every child to be fed
And every person to have a bed
And for the world to stop spilling red

The Song of Life

<u>Best Friend</u>

A person to relate
They are your
Best mates
Things between you
Are great

If you're deaf
And the other can't speak
If you were friends
I'd guarantee
You could scratch each other's backs

You're like two gourmet chefs
That's what makes you unique

The times get tough
And a bit rough
You'll probably
Just laugh it off

Peyush Gurung

And maybe even
Help each other
On the way

Best of friends
Until death departs
But still memories
Living within
Undying hearts

About the Author

Author, Peyush Gurung, was born in April 2004 in Nepal. He flew to England when he was three years old. Then he left England after three years to spend another two years in Brunei because his father was in the British Army and had to work there. He then flew back to England and he started to open up to the world of literature when he entered a poem competition in Coombes CE Primary School, Reading. Though he did not win, he was very proud of his work and was motivated to make more poems.

After two more years, he moved to Dartford, Kent, and he started to write and read more. Two years later he was on the move again, this time to High Wycombe where he continued to write poems and participate in competitions. His poems were included in The Poetry Trails book, *Money*, which is a great book. Some of his poems were also published in the Greenwich Times magazine! He has also entered competitions such as national poetry and ghost stories.

He was awarded certificates for arts, spelling, writing poems and reading, medals mostly bronze, and he also won an award – Master Builder – for a Shakespeare house design building competition.